"...for fragments of light
in the darkness"

# Beyond

# the stars

# Introduction

Grief is a journey no one chooses to take, yet sooner or later we all find ourselves walking this unfamiliar path. We lose loved ones, friends, and even pets who have shared precious fragments of our lives with us. It is an experience that shakes us to the core, often leaving us with more questions than answers, with a void that seems unfillable.

The five stages of grief - **Denial, Anger, Negotiation, Depression, and Acceptance** - describe the emotional journeys we go through after a loss. However, they don't always follow a linear path. We may relive a stage we've already gone through, or jump from one to another without warning. This journey doesn't have a precise map; everyone finds their own unique path. There's no right or wrong way to grieve, just a way that's unique to you.

**"Beyond the stars"** was created to accompany you on this journey, not to provide you with solutions or definitive answers, but to offer you a space in which to recognize and give voice to your feelings.

Poetry, with its ability to express what we often fail to say with everyday words, becomes a powerful tool for processing grief. This book does not pretend to tell you how to overcome grief, but it offers you fragments of light to go through it, with delicacy and respect for your experience.

# The five stages of grief

The stages of grief, described by psychiatrist Elisabeth Kübler-Ross, represent an emotional map, but they should not be seen as obligatory stages.

Each stage reflects a part of our inner journey:

**Denial:** the refusal to accept the reality of loss, a temporary refuge from the truth.

**Anger:** the explosion of emotions that seeks a culprit, someone or something on which to unload the pain.

**Negotiation:** The attempt to negotiate with fate, life, or God, desperately trying to reverse a loss.

**Depression:** the confrontation with the void left by the loved one, a deep sadness that permeates everything.

**Acceptance:** the awareness that, even while living with pain, we can find a new balance.

Each stage helps us recognize parts of our grief and integrate them into our experience. In this book, we will explore each of them through poems that capture the emotional essence of these moments, offering you a safe space where grief can be expressed, understood, and shared.

# Poetry and mourning: a universal language

Poetry was chosen because, in moments of profound sorrow, everyday language often falls short. When words seem unable to capture the depth of pain, poetry offers a way to express the unspoken.

With its ability to condense deep emotions into a few lines, poetry resonates in a way that speaks directly to the heart. The poems in "Beyond the Stars" do not aim to explain or solve but to reflect your feelings, gently guiding you through the five stages of grief.

This collection is a journey that explores not only pain but also the possibility of hope. Each poem is a fragment of solace, a small beacon illuminating the path toward acceptance and inner peace.

**"Beyond the Stars"** doesn't refer to a far-off place but rather an inward journey. It's an invitation to look beyond the pain, to find strength and meaning even in the most challenging times.

Whether you are currently grieving or have experienced loss in the past, **"Beyond the Stars"** offers a safe space to rediscover yourself through words and reflection.

# The importance of reflection

In addition to the poems, this book offers you a personal space for reflection. At the end of each section, you will find reflective questions that invite you to explore your relationship with grief and the emotions you are experiencing. These questions are not an obligation, but an opportunity for those who wish to actively process their grief. Writing, just like poetry, can become a powerful tool for healing and self-exploration.

Now, before we begin our journey, I invite you to take a moment to reflect on what you have read so far. These questions are not seeking definitive answers, but are intended to provide a safe space for you to delve into your emotions and personal experiences.

*How do you feel about the idea of exploring grief through poetry? Do you think it can help you process emotions that you have not been able to express until now?*

*Is there a stage of grief that you think you've already experienced? How did that moment affect you, and what emotions did it leave you with?*

_____

_____

_____

_____

_____

*What role does writing play in your life?*
*Have you ever found relief or comfort by putting your thoughts and feelings on paper?*

_____

_____

_____

_____

_____

*How do you think reading poetry can help you connect with your own pain or that of others? Have you ever found comfort in sharing your emotions through art or literature?*

_____

_____

_____

_____

_____

*Exploring grief can be a difficult process. Is there anything you fear about going through on this journey? What thoughts or emotions do you think might arise as you reflect on your journey?*

_____

_____

_____

_____

_____

*"I cling to the silence,
hoping it's just a dream.
But the dream doesn't
answer me either."*

# Denial

# A temporary refuge from the reality of pain

When we face a significant loss, many people's first reaction is often to deny the reality of what happened. Denial is an instinctive and natural response: a defense mechanism that the mind activates to protect itself from the immediate and devastating impact of grief. It is as if the mind refuses to accept the severity of the loss, trying to maintain a sense of normalcy that, however, no longer exists.

Denial works as a kind of emotional anesthetic. In those first moments of shock, the mind tries to delay the confrontation with the full weight of the suffering, offering us a momentary respite. This phase can last days, weeks, or even months, and in some cases it can manifest only in fits and starts, as an intermittent feeling of unreality. It is common to experience grief as if it were a dream, where the mind oscillates between acceptance of reality and the hope that everything will go back to the way it was before.

In this sense, denial is not a sign of weakness or inability to deal with pain. It is a resource that temporarily protects the person from immediate trauma, giving them the time they need to prepare themselves to deal with pain gradually.

In many cultures, there is a lot of pressure to "be strong" or "get over" the loss quickly, but denial reminds us that everyone has their own time. During this stage, we may reject reality with phrases like "It can't be" or "It couldn't have happened to me," trying to avoid a direct confrontation with the truth.

Denial can take many forms. In some cases, it can manifest itself as a complete denial of reality, a way of avoiding accepting that the loved one will never return. Some may continue to live as if nothing has changed, actively avoiding any thought or conversation that forces them to deal with the loss. This denial may be accompanied by habitual gestures, such as leaving the deceased's things exactly as they were, continuing to behave as if he or she were still present. In these moments, the mind takes refuge in normalcy, even though the heart knows that everything has changed.

However, denial can be even more subtle. Many people, while rationally accepting that the loss has occurred, avoid dealing with the deeper emotions that come with it. Instead of crying or expressing their grief openly, they focus on everyday activities, trying to maintain a routine that distracts them from the inner turmoil. It is a form of emotional denial, in which the mind seems to know what has happened, but the heart is not yet ready to deal with it.

This behavior is a defense that helps us not to be overwhelmed by pain all at once.

One of the most difficult aspects of denial is that, in a way, it can be helpful. By protecting the person from the acute pain of loss, it allows for a gradual adjustment to the new reality. Without this phase, the trauma of the loss may be too intense to bear all at once. Denial gives the mind moments of respite, emotional breathing spaces, allowing the individual to approach the pain little by little. It is as if the mind builds a temporary barrier to prevent the immediate and overwhelming suffering, allowing the person to slowly prepare to face it.

However, denial cannot last forever. If it continues for too long, it can become an obstacle to the healing process. The inability to accept the reality of the loss can prevent the individual from undertaking the necessary grieving process. When denial becomes an insurmountable wall, the person can remain stuck in a sort of limbo, unable to move forward. This is the point at which the initial defense mechanism, which was intended to be temporary, turns into an emotional prison, preventing the person from facing reality and healing.

It's important to remember that not everyone experiences denial the same way. Some people may only spend a few hours in this stage, while others may remain in it for days, weeks, or even months. Additionally, you may swing back and forth between denial and other stages of grief, such as anger or depression.

This constant movement between different stages is a common feature of grief, which never follows a linear or predictable path. During this stage, the reality of the loss may seem too painful to face. The person may feel stuck, unable to accept that life has changed forever. This sense of immobility can be frustrating for those close to the grieving person, but it is essential to understand that denial is a natural part of the grieving process. It is a temporary phase, which eventually fades when the mind is ready to deal with the trauma of the loss.

During this time, emotional support can play a crucial role. People who are in denial do not need to be forced to accept reality, but rather to be listened to and supported. It is important to offer an understanding and silent presence, allowing the person to live this phase without feeling judged or pressured. Denial disappears when the person is ready to confront the pain, and this only happens when they feel safe and supported in doing so.

Furthermore, denial does not only manifest itself on a mental or emotional level. The body can also react with physical symptoms, such as a feeling of dizziness, difficulty concentrating, or a general sense of detachment from reality. These symptoms can be seen as a sign that the mind and body are processing the loss in their own way, trying to protect themselves from the immediate trauma.

Over time, the denial begins to dissolve, like a fog that slowly clears. As the mind begins to accept the reality of the loss, other, more intense emotions emerge, such as anger or deep sadness. This transition is not easy, but it is a necessary step in order to begin the healing process. It is at this point that the pain begins to be felt more acutely, but it is also a sign that the person is ready to face it.

Denial, therefore, is a necessary and temporary phase, an emotional pause that allows us to deal with pain gradually. It does not mean that the person does not understand the gravity of the loss, but that he or she needs time to prepare to fully accept it. It is a natural defense mechanism, which protects the mind until it is ready to face reality.

As grief progresses, acceptance of the loss becomes inevitable, but that does not mean the pain disappears. Healing begins when the person is able to embrace reality, acknowledging both the pain and the possibility of continuing to live despite the loss.

# Gradually accepting reality

At this stage, it is normal to feel confused and unready to accept the reality of the loss. Denial is a natural defense mechanism that allows us to absorb the pain in small steps.

## Advice:

- **Give yourself time**: Don't force yourself to accept everything immediately. Let reality unfold over time.

- **Talk to someone**: Even if it seems difficult, sharing your feelings with a trusted person can help you acknowledge reality without feeling overwhelmed.

- **Write down your thoughts**: Putting your feelings down on paper can help you process the loss slowly.

- **Take it one step at a time**: You don't have to deal with all the pain at once. Take small aspects of reality, day by day.

- **Accept the need to deny**: Don't feel guilty about denial, it's part of the process. You can go through this phase without rushing.

## A Thin Veil

A thin veil
separates me from the world,
reality speaks,
but I don't hear it.

—————————— ∞ ——————————

## Shadow of the Day

I walk among shadows
that have no name,
days that pass,
but I remain still.

**The Still Time**

Time stands still,
like a frozen hourglass,
grains of sand suspended
in the void of waiting.

Everything remains still,
as if tomorrow
could still come.

But tomorrow will not come,
yet I cling to
this fragile illusion.

In the silence,
I wait for a signal,
a shadow,
a heartbeat that
isn't there.

**It is not true**

It can't be true,
this pain isn't real.
I still wait for your voice,
but silence answers me.

## Shadows at the Door

The door is ajar,
a crack of hope.
I wait for your shadow,
but no one passes,
no one calls.

## In a Dream

I'm in a dream
that I can't wake up from.

Your face appears,
hazy like morning mist,
yet I believe that
if I closed my eyes just a moment longer,
I could touch you again.

In a room of light,
in my mind,
you are still there,
still and perfect.

**Beyond the Glass**

I look at the world beyond the glass,
distorted, distant, unreal.
I touch the cold surface,
but I can't feel,
as if life were just a reflection.

**To vanish**

I don't want to hear,
I don't want to know.
I close my eyes
and wait for the world
to dissolve.

## Waves of Silence

I let time slip by
like distant waves on the sea.
I tell myself that it's not true,
that everything will go back
to the way it was before.
But the sea does not stop,
the waves do not stop.

Every day we move
a little further away
from who we were.
And I remain here,
still on the shore,
waiting for you,
knowing that you will not come.

Hope keeps me tied
to this infinite water,
as the waves wash away
every trace of your passage.

## Calling the Void

I call your name,
but the echo fades into
the void that surrounds me.
I seek your presence
in the long silences,
in the fleeting shadows.
Yet I persist.
Maybe, if I call loud enough,
the void will answer.

## Between Knowing and Ignoring

I'm torn
between not wanting to know
and knowing too much.
In the middle,
only silence remains.

## The Impossible Return

I await your return
as one awaits spring
after a long winter.

Every day I tell myself
that maybe today is the day,
the day when everything will change,
when the cold will vanish
and life will return.

But winter doesn't end,
and you don't come back.

And yet, I can't stop believing,
dreaming that, perhaps,
in a different tomorrow,
everything will be as before.

## The Sea of Distance

Your absence is
a sea too vast,
an ocean I cannot cross.

They tell me to accept it,
that everything passes.

But I remain here,
motionless on the shore,
watching the waves go away,
never returning.

Yet, every night,
I wonder if beyond the horizon,
in an unknown port,
your distant voice
can still resonate.

## The Moment Before

I always relive
the moment before,
when the future
was still possible,
when everything
could still change.

## A Suspended Gesture

I remain here,
an unfinished gesture,
a word never said.
If only I could stop time,
if only I could go back,
maybe everything would make sense.
But time flies,
and I remain stuck
in its silent flow.

## A World of Memories

I live in a parallel world
where you never left.
That's where I find you,
among the blurry memories
of what we were.

## The Shadow of the Voice

Your voice is a shadow
that always escapes
when I try to touch it.

## The Infinite Dream

Every night I dream
that nothing has changed,
that you are still here.

In the dream, we talk as always,
I laugh at your jokes,
I listen to your stories.

But every time I wake up,
reality hits me.

Between sleep and wakefulness,
I delude myself for a moment
that you could still be beside me.

But when I open my eyes,
the room is empty.

Yet, I continue to dream,
because it is the only place
where you still exist.

## A Safe Silence

In the imagined silence
I find shelter,
a place where the world
cannot enter.

Here, you do not exist,
but neither does your absence,
like a void that fills the air,
without ever touching the heart.

It's a pause,
a held breath,
a fragile refuge,
before everything collapses.

The voices die down,
the thoughts stop,
and an unreal calm envelops me,
an illusion that protects me
from what I know is coming.

In this safe silence,
time does not pass,
every second remains suspended,
chained to the hope
that nothing will ever change.

I cling to this quiet,
pretending that, perhaps,
reality will never come knocking.

But I know it's only a matter of time.
Eventually, the silence will break,
the invisible walls will fall,
and I will have to face the world
I've tried to hide.

But for now, in this silence,
I am safe,
protected by the weight of the truth
that I cannot yet bear.

## Shadow of Fog

A thick fog
envelops my heart.
Every step is unreal,
as if the world were
just a distant dream.
I tell myself it can't be true,
that I'll wake up tomorrow,
but the fog remains,
unchanged and silent.

## Existing Without You

I exist in your absence,
a reflection of who we were.
The world around me moves,
but I remain still,
motionless in memory.
I don't want to let you go,
I don't want to admit that
you're never coming back.

*What was your first reaction to the news of the loss? How did you experience those initial moments?*

---

---

---

---

---

---

*Was there a part of you that struggled to accept the reality of the loss? What thoughts or feelings led you to deny what had happened?*

---

---

---

---

---

*Have you ever had moments when you felt like everything was just a bad dream? How did you react when reality came back?*

_____

_____

_____

_____

_____

_____

*How have you avoided facing the reality of the loss?*
*Have you found yourself seeking distractions or retreating into everyday activities?*

_____

_____

_____

_____

_____

_____

*Have you ever tried to convince yourself that the loss wasn't real, perhaps waiting for signs that everything would go back to normal? What emotions did you experience as you tried to hold on to that hope?*

*What helped you begin to recognize the reality of grief? Was there a moment or experience that allowed you to at least partially accept the loss?*

# Meditation exercise: The first step towards acceptance

- Sit comfortably, close your eyes and take a deep breath. Bring your attention to your body and notice where you feel tension.

- Imagine a door in front of you. Behind that door is the reality of loss. You don't have to open it right away; you can just lean into it.

- Repeat to yourself: "*I am not ready for everything, but I can accept a little at a time.*"

- Imagine a ray of light filtering through the door, gently caressing you. This ray reminds you that, even in the harshest reality, there is a thread of hope.

- Inhale slowly and think, "*I take one step at a time.*" Exhale and release some resistance. Repeat for 5 breath cycles.

- When you feel ready, imagine opening the door a little, just enough to welcome what you can handle today.

*"I cry out to the sky
without receiving an answer,
yet my anger rises
like a storm in my heart."*

# Anger

# A fire that burns in the heart of mourning

After the denial phase, when the reality of the loss begins to dawn, many people enter the second stage of grief: anger. This stage brings with it an explosion of intense and often chaotic emotions. Unable to accept the injustice of the loss, the mind searches for someone to blame, and anger becomes a natural response to the frustration and helplessness felt in the face of an incomprehensible reality.

Anger can come in many forms. Some people get angry at themselves, blaming themselves for not doing enough. Others direct their anger at those around them, even for no real reason. Sometimes, this anger can even be directed at the person who died, blaming them for leaving those left behind to suffer. Although these feelings may seem irrational or uncomfortable, they are part of the natural grieving process.

During this phase, it is common to ask yourself, "Why did this happen to me?" or "Why now?" The mind tries to make sense of what seems senseless, but often this search only leads to further frustration. When answers do not come, anger becomes a release valve for the enormous emotional pressure that has built up.

One of the most difficult aspects of anger is that it can seem unfair, both to the person experiencing it and to the person being affected. Emotional outbursts may seem disproportionate or directed at someone who is not at fault. However, it is important to remember that this anger is not intentionally directed at those close to you, but rather represents an attempt to give form to an emotion that would otherwise be too painful to handle.

Anger can also be directed at abstract entities, such as life, fate, or even God. Some people may feel betrayed by their faith, wondering how a higher power could allow such great suffering. This spiritual crisis is an expression of the internal struggle to make sense of the loss, and is a natural aspect of the anger phase.

Despite its destructive nature, anger plays an important role in the healing process. It is an active emotion that, although painful, marks the beginning of the confrontation with the reality of grief. If denial serves to protect from pain, anger is the first sign that one is beginning to recognize the loss. It is a necessary, albeit turbulent, step toward acceptance.

However, it is important to find a healthy outlet for anger. If not expressed appropriately, it can strain relationships and further isolate the grieving person. Repressed feelings can turn into resentment or lead to depression. For this reason, it is essential to find constructive ways to channel anger, allowing the person to release the burden without harming themselves or others.

Typical behaviors of this stage include irritability, sudden emotional outbursts, and a constant sense of injustice. Anger may also be projected onto situations that are apparently unrelated to the loss, such as work problems or difficulties in relationships. This happens because the person is still processing their grief and seeks outlets in other areas of life.

It is important to remember that anger is not just a negative emotion. It can also be seen as a form of energy, an attempt by the mind to react to trauma. As painful as anger is, it restores a sense of control and power. Loss leaves us feeling helpless, and anger, for all its intensity, represents the will to oppose this helplessness.

Don't judge yourself for your anger. Feeling angry doesn't mean you're evil or selfish, nor does it diminish your love for the person who has passed away. Anger is a natural part of grieving, and acknowledging it, accepting it, and finding ways to express it in healthy ways are essential steps in moving forward on the healing journey.

This stage does not follow a linear path: you may go from anger to denial or depression and then back to anger. This movement between different emotions is perfectly normal, since mourning is a complex and irregular process.

For those close to a grieving person, dealing with the anger phase can be difficult. It is essential to remember that the anger is not intentionally directed at them. Listening, without judging or trying to fix, can make a big difference. Often, those who are angry just need to be understood and accepted.

Over time, anger gradually loses its intensity. As the reality of the loss is internalized, the person begins to move into other phases, such as negotiation or depression, where emotions are less explosive but just as deep. Anger is a necessary stage, marking the beginning of the healing process.

In conclusion, the phase of anger in grief, as painful as it is, is a sign that the person is starting to deal with their pain. Embracing this emotion, understanding it and finding healthy ways to express it, is essential to allow the healing process to move forward. Just like a fire that burns brightly, anger can leave scars, but it is also a sign of transformation and inner growth.

# Expressing emotion in a constructive way

Anger is a common and natural response to loss. You may feel angry at yourself, at others, or even at the person who is no longer with you. It is important not to bottle up this anger, but to find healthy ways to express it.

## Advice:

- **Give voice to your anger:** Write a letter (even if you never send it) expressing everything that makes you angry.

- **Find a physical outlet**: Doing physical activity like walking, running, or even hitting a pillow can help release built-up tension.

- **Talk to someone you trust**: Sharing your anger can ease the burden you feel, even if it seems irrational.

- **Accept that anger is temporary**: Even if it feels overwhelming now, anger won't last forever. Allow yourself to feel it without judging yourself.

- **Create Something**: Use art, writing, or music to transform anger into creative expression.

**Flame of Rage**

A flame grows,
devours every thought,
I want to shout to the sky,
but the sky is far away, deaf.

**Why?**

Why me?
The world doesn't respond,
and my anger
remains faceless.

## The Injustice of Death

Death is a thief,
he took everything from me
without asking,
without warning.

And I remain here,
alone,
raising my fists
against a sky
that doesn't listen.

Where were you
when I needed you?
Where were you
when the world collapsed
beneath my feet?

## Furious Wind

Like a furious wind,
anger blows on
the rubble of my heart.
Everything breaks,
everything bends.
I wish the wind
would take everything away,
but I remain here,
with my fist closed
against infinity.

## Screaming into the Void

I screamed at the void,
but the void responded
only with silence.

## Game of Destiny

Cruel fate,
you took from me what I loved
without mercy,
without warning.

If only I could,
I would have challenged you,
but I am only a man,
a prisoner of your shadow.

Now only anger remains,
it burns inside me
like a flame that never goes out,
that leaves me no peace.

## Inner Storm

A storm inside me
screams its fury to the world.
I can't stop it,
I can't control it.
Anger eats me from the inside,
without respite,
without breathing.

And all I can do is
let it explode,
let it spill over into those around me,
even if they don't deserve it.
My anger has no boundaries,
it knows no limits.

But when the storm subsides,
nothing remains.
Only destruction,
only a void that screams louder
than the storm itself.

**Fire that Devours**

The fire of anger
devours my heart,
every flame consumes,
and nothing remains,
only ashes.

**The Fist Against the Wall**

I hit the wall,
but it didn't respond.
My hands burn,
but the pain doesn't go away.

**Betrayed by Life**

Life has betrayed me,
like a friend who turns
his back on you.
And I remain here,
staring into the abyss.

**Thunder in the Heart**

There is a thunder in my heart,
it explodes every time
I think of you.
I can't stop him,
I can't calm him down.

## Ocean of Rage

I am a castaway
in an ocean of anger.

Every wave pushes me
further from the shore,
every splash of water
drags me down.

I look for a hold,
I look for a way out,
but there is no shore,
there is no salvation.

I am alone in this sea,
fighting against a destiny
I cannot control.

**Unjust Void**

You left me with a void
that I can't fill.
It's unfair,
it's cruel.

❍

**No Justice**

There is no justice in this pain.
I searched for answers,
but found only emptiness.
Every blow I deal to fate
bounces off an invisible wall.
My anger is helpless,
but I can't let it go.
Not yet.

**Against the Sky**

I cry out to the sky
that has taken away from me
what I loved,
but the sky remains still,
indifferent to my pain.

How can he be so distant,
so insensitive?
My heart screams,
but the sky is silent.

**Cage of Rage**

I'm trapped in a cage
made of my own anger.
And I can't get out of it.

**The Silenced Scream**

Inside me,
there is a scream that I cannot express.
I want to scream to the world, scream to you,
but the words get stuck in my throat,
suffocated by anger.
Every time I try to speak,
only tears come out.

And this anger finds no peace,
no place to rest.
It's like a wounded animal,
writhing in pain,
trying to break free
from a cage it can't see.

It's not fair,
it's not fair that you're no longer here,
that the world continues to turn
as if nothing had happened.
And here I am,
stuck in this cage of pain,
with no way out.

51

**The Power of Silence**

The silence around me
is louder than my screams.
I scream,
I get agitated,
I try to break through this wall,
but the silence remains,
motionless,
while my anger
is consumed into nothingness.

**Wind of Pain**

Every breath of wind
reminds me of your name,
and my anger grows,
like an approaching storm.

## The Anger of the Heart

My heart is a battlefield,
where anger and pain
clash relentlessly.
There is no winner,
there is no defeat,
 just an endless struggle,
a cycle that repeats itself,
day after day.

Every beat is a blow,
every breath is an assault.
And I no longer know what to fight,
I no longer know who the enemy is,
if it is inside me,
or outside,
in a world that I no longer recognize.

My anger blinds me,
distances me from those who love me,
builds walls around me,
high and insurmountable.

It holds me prisoner,
while the world moves on,
while everything I know
crumbles under the weight of this pain,
this invisible war
that only I can feel.

But one day,
maybe,
the battle will end.
Maybe one day my heart
will find peace,
a truce in the turmoil.

But not today,
not now.

For now, I remain here,
fighting against what I cannot change,
against a destiny I cannot stop,
and against myself,
which I cannot let go.

*Did you feel angry following the loss?*
*If so, towards whom or what did you direct this anger?*

*How has your anger affected your relationships with others?*
*Have there been times when you felt frustrated or isolated*
*because of your anger?*

*Have you ever felt anger towards the missing person? If so, how did you deal with this feeling?*

*What helped you vent your anger? Have you found constructive ways to express this emotion?*

*Has your anger manifested itself in unexpected ways or in situations that would not normally elicit such emotions? How did you handle these moments and what did you learn about yourself through these experiences?*

*Looking back, how do you perceive your anger now?*
*Do you think this was a necessary step in your healing process?*

# Meditation exercise:
# The fire that heals

- Close your eyes and imagine that you are near a fire. This fire represents your anger: hot, intense, but contained.

- Place your hands over your heart and breathe slowly, feeling your heart rate. Repeat, *"My anger has a place, but it doesn't define me."*

- Imagine throwing everything that torments you into the fire: the unsaid words, the injustices, the pain. Watch the fire transform everything into heat and light.

- Inhale and think, *"I am free from the burden of anger."* Exhale and let go of the destructive energy. Continue for 5 breaths.

- When the fire calms down, imagine a small, gentle flame remaining, a positive force that will guide you forward.

*"If only I could
rewind time,
rewind every moment,
maybe I could find a way
to have you still here."*

# Negotiation

# The attempt to regain control over pain

After the emotional outburst of anger, many grieving people move into a more reflective phase: negotiation. In this third stage of grief, one desperately tries to negotiate with reality, as if it were possible to make a deal to reverse or mitigate the loss. The mind tries to find a compromise, attempting to rewrite the past through hypothetical thoughts and wishes.

During this phase, people often ask themselves: "If only I had done something differently, maybe all this wouldn't have happened", or "If only I had had more time..." These thoughts reflect the need to exert some control over a situation that, in reality, is completely beyond our control. It is an attempt to make sense of the loss, a search for explanations that can make the pain more bearable.

Negotiation can also take on a spiritual dimension. Some turn to God or fate, trying to make a pact: "If I do this, maybe I will get back what I lost." Although irrational, this type of thinking is a way of seeking hope and comfort in the face of what seems unbearable. The mind, at this time, is still in a phase of resistance, not ready to accept the irreversibility of the loss.

One of the most common aspects of negotiation is guilt. Grieving people may begin to blame themselves for actions they could not have controlled: "If only I had been more present," or "If only I had acted sooner." This guilt, although irrational, represents the mind's attempt to make sense of a situation that defies logic.

Negotiation can also manifest itself through a constant obsession with the details of the past. You try to retrace every moment, every decision, hoping to pinpoint the point where things "went wrong." This constant thinking can become exhausting, as it tries to solve a problem that, in reality, has no solution.

Another aspect of negotiation is the desire to go back in time. Some people retreat into thoughts or dreams of a past in which the loss never occurred, creating an alternate reality in which everything is fine. This desire to escape the present prolongs the acceptance process, as it postpones the confrontation with the reality of the pain.

Despite its irrational nature, negotiation is closely linked to hope. Even when we know rationally that the loss is final, the mind clings to the idea that there is still a chance to change things. This hope allows us to face grief one step at a time, even knowing that there is no real compromise.

As with other stages of grief, negotiation does not follow a linear path. You may oscillate between this stage and other stages, such as anger or depression, in an irregular way. Each person experiences grief in a unique way, and negotiation can manifest itself in different ways for each person.

For those who support a grieving person, it is important to understand that negotiation is not a rationalization of the loss, but an attempt to temporarily deal with the pain. Forcing the person to confront reality right away can be counterproductive. Instead, offering a nonjudgmental listening ear and support is essential at this time.

Over time, negotiation loses its power. As the grieving person approaches the next stage, depression, he or she begins to face the reality of the loss more directly. The desire to change what has happened gives way to deeper sadness and gradual acceptance. Negotiation, then, is an intermediate step that prepares the mind to deal with grief more fully.

In conclusion, the negotiation phase is a natural stage in the grieving process. Although irrational, it is an attempt by the mind to find an escape from the pain, to regain some control. Accepting it as part of the journey is essential, as it allows the grieving person to explore their pain in a reflective way, gradually moving closer to acceptance and healing.

# Recognizing that the past cannot be changed

Negotiation is a phase in which you try to make hypothetical agreements with yourself, fate, or a higher power, in the hope of reversing the loss. It is a phase full of "if onlys" and "should haves," which can generate a lot of frustration.

## Advice:

- **Recognize your limitations**: You can't change what happened. Accepting this fact can help you stop looking for unrealistic answers.

- **Forgive yourself**: Guilt is common at this stage, but it is important to remember that no one can control every event in life.

- **Face the present**: Focus your thoughts on what you can do now, instead of getting stuck in what you can no longer change.

- **Talk to someone who can listen without judging**: Sharing your negotiation thoughts with an understanding person can help you see them from a different perspective.

- **Make a list of what you can still do**: Even if you can't bring back the past, you can find ways to honor the person's memory and move on with your life.

**Be Alone**

If only I had known,
if only I had acted sooner,
maybe you would be here now,
maybe I would not be lost in this void.

**Exchanges**

What would I give to have a moment back,
I would exchange every certainty of mine,
every fragment of the future
for another chance to change everything.

## A Silent Wish

I ask the sky,
but I do it in silence.
There is no prayer,
just a wish that flows
between the unspoken words.

What would I give
to have back a moment,
a breath,
a fragment of what was.

Maybe if I had known
what I know now,
things would be different.

Maybe if I could go back
I could fix it.

## Promises to Destiny

I promise fate
that I will do better,
if only it could give me
another chance.

## Invisible Coins

I paid invisible coins
to buy a moment,
but time does not sell,
does not listen,
does not stop.

## Contract with the Infinite

I made a contract with infinity,
I offered it my heart,
my soul,
everything I am,
in exchange for a single instant.

I asked for the past back,
a past I can't forget.
I promised to be different,
to change everything.
But the infinite remains silent,
leaving me hanging,
without answers.

And while I wait for a miracle,
time continues to flow,
unaltered and indifferent.
And I'm left here,
with my unsigned contract.

**In the Hands**

I tried to hold you
like sand in my hands,
but time slips away,
relentless and deaf to my pain.
I tell myself that I could have done more,
but the past doesn't listen.

**Your Voice in the Wind**

I search for your voice in the wind,
hoping that it can bring me
a message,
a sign that can change the present.
But the wind blows without answers,
and my heart remains empty,
without that word that
could save everything.

## The Dance of Time

Time dances around me,
but I can't follow it.

I tried to negotiate,
to stop it,
to change its pace,
but time doesn't listen.

I asked him for a truce,
a break,
to reflect,
to go back and do things differently.

But time is deaf,
it does not answer my pleas.

And so I stand here,
watching her dance,
knowing that there is nothing I can do about it,
knowing that even if I offer everything I have,
nothing will change.

### If I Could

If I could have just one moment,
one breath suspended in time,
I would change every unsaid word,
every missed gesture.
I would be there, with you,
giving shape to everything
that remained incomplete.

Maybe if I could go back,
I could reverse fate
and erase this pain.

### Another Day

I ask the wind
to give me another day,
but the wind passes by,
without answering.

## The Agreement That Does Not Exist

I sought a deal
with the universe,
a secret pact to trade this pain
for a second chance.

But the universe is silent,
indifferent to my attempts.

The past remains immobile,
like a painting in which
I can no longer paint.

And I remain here,
begging the void
that cannot answer.

## Trading the Pain

I would trade my pain
for a smile.
I would go back in time
if I could do it all over again.

---

## Shadows of a Possible Past

I live in the shadows
of a possible past,
a past that never was
but could have been.
If only I had taken a different step,
said a different word,
perhaps everything would have changed today.
But the shadows remain,
suspended between what is
and what could have been.

## The Unspoken Words

There are words
I have never said,
words that now scream
inside me,
looking for a way out.

I repeat them in my mind,
hoping that,
somehow,
they can reach you.

Maybe
if you had said them before,
you would be here now.

Maybe,
they would have changed destiny.

## The Price of Forgiveness

If I could pay the price of forgiveness,
I would do so without hesitation.
But fate doesn't sell forgiveness,
only memories.

## The Lost Days

Every lost day
is a burden I carry,
a regret I can't shake.
If only I could go back,
maybe I could change everything.

## Invisible Offers

I have offered everything,
every breath,
every thought,
to an unresponsive fate.

I sat down
at the negotiation table,
but no one on the other side
accepted my offers.

The past is immovable,
and I remain here,
offering what I do not have,
to try to change
what I cannot touch.

## If I Were

If I had been there,
if I had known,
if I had said…
but time does not change
for my assumptions.

— ∞ —

## The Weight of Choices

Every choice weighs,
like a stone sinking in water.
I wonder if I could have changed course,
if I had acted differently,
if I had chosen better,
maybe I wouldn't be here,
regretting the past.

## A Second Life

What would I give for a second life,
a life where I could do everything right,
where every mistake would be erased
and every unspoken word would
finally find a voice.

In that life,
you would still be here,
next to me,
and time would be kind,
allowing us to live
every moment without regrets.

But this life doesn't exist,
it's just a dream
that lulls me when the pain is too strong.
A dream that holds me prisoner,
while the real world
continues to flow mercilessly.

*Have you ever tried to mentally renegotiate the loss?*
*Have you had thoughts like, "if only I had... then things would have been different"?*

_____

_____

_____

_____

_____

_____

*Were there times when you held on to the hope that you could change what happened?*
*If so, what thoughts or prayers did you address to yourself or to a higher power?*

_____

_____

_____

_____

_____

_____

*Did you experience feelings of guilt during this phase?*
*If so, how did you deal with these feelings?*

*How do you feel about the decisions you made before the loss?*
*Are there things you wish you would have done differently, or*
*have you found peace with the past?*

*Have you ever felt the need to search for a "why" or meaning in the loss? If so, how has it affected the way you grieve and search for answers?*

_____

_____

_____

_____

_____

_____

*What helped you realize that you couldn't change the situation? Was it a gradual process or a specific moment that brought you to this realization?*

_____

_____

_____

_____

_____

_____

# Meditation exercise:
# The present is all I have

- Sit in a quiet place and breathe deeply. Bring your attention to the present moment.

- Imagine a sky full of stars. Each star represents an "if only": "If only I had done more." "If only I could go back."

- Repeat to yourself: "*I cannot change the past, but I can honor it.*"

- Inhale and imagine the sky starting to lighten. The stars disappear one by one, leaving a clear and serene sky.

- With each exhalation, release a regret. Repeat, "*The past cannot be changed, but my love remains.*"

- When you are ready, imagine looking up and seeing the sun rise, symbolizing the new day that awaits you.

"Sadness is a deep abyss,
but even in its darkness
I am beginning
to see a path."

# Depression

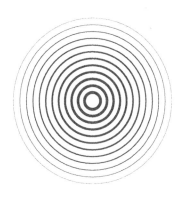

# The emptiness and deep sadness of loss

The fourth stage of grief, depression, is perhaps the most painful and difficult to deal with. After denying the reality of the loss, after the anger and attempts to negotiate with fate, one arrives at the rawest awareness of grief. It is here that the person really begins to confront the void left by the loss and the deep sadness that comes from it.

Depression in grief, while having some similarities to clinical depression, is a natural and temporary reaction to loss. In this phase, melancholy permeates every aspect of daily life. The realization that life has changed irrevocably, and that nothing will ever be the same again, comes painfully and inevitably.

During this stage, you often feel overwhelmed by emptiness. Things that once gave you pleasure may seem insignificant. You may feel detached from the world, as if you are trapped in a bubble of sadness that you cannot escape. It is no longer a time to look for answers or solutions, but to accept the reality of the loss and deal with the pain that comes with it.

One of the most difficult aspects of depression in grief is loneliness. Even when surrounded by loved ones, it can feel incredibly lonely, because no one can fully understand the individual pain that one is feeling. This sense of isolation can lead to emotional withdrawal, where the grieving person retreats further into their own internal world.

The depression phase is often accompanied by a sense of loss of hope. After trying to change things in the negotiation phase, one comes to understand that nothing can bring back the loved one. This leads to a painful surrender, in which one accepts that the loss is final. The awareness of this irreversibility can leave the person in a state of deep desolation.

Depression in grief can manifest itself in different ways. Some people cry frequently and withdraw from daily activities, while others become apathetic, losing interest in everything they once loved. This sense of apathy reflects the difficulty of finding meaning in life after the loss.

One of the most pervasive aspects of depression is fatigue, both emotional and physical. The weight of grief can seem unbearable, and even the simplest tasks can become difficult to cope with. This fatigue comes from the intensity of emotions and the difficulty of finding purpose in life after the loss.

At this stage, guilt may resurface. You may blame yourself for not having done enough or not having said everything you wanted to say. These regrets can further fuel your depression, making it harder to see a way out. However, it is important to remember that grieving is a complicated process and there is no right or wrong way to deal with it.

A common mistake is to think that depression in grief must be "overcome" quickly. In reality, it is a crucial phase in healing. It is the time when the person begins to deeply process the pain and come to terms with the new reality. Although it is painful, it is necessary in order to reach acceptance.

Crying is an important part of depression. Crying allows you to physically express your pain and provides temporary relief. Although it may seem debilitating, it is a natural healing mechanism that helps release the intensity of your emotions. During this phase, it is essential that the grieving person not feel judged for their pain or difficulty "moving on."

Deep reflection is another aspect of depression in grief. The person may spend a lot of time thinking about the deceased, reliving happy or painful moments. This is not only a sign of nostalgia, but a way to keep the memory alive and accept that, even if physically absent, the loved one continues to live in memories.

Although depression is a painful stage, it is often a prelude to acceptance. As you grieve, you begin to make room for the idea that life can go on. It is not about "getting over" the loss, but about learning to live with it. Depression is a necessary step toward a new understanding of life and loss.

For those who care for a grieving person, it is important to offer support, even if it may seem like words are not enough. Being present, listening without judgment, and offering silent comfort can make a big difference. Even if the grieving person feels isolated, knowing that they are not alone can be a great help.

There is no set time to overcome the phase of depression. Some go through it in a few weeks, others in months or years. It can also recur at particular times, such as anniversaries or holidays. However, it is an inevitable and crucial part of the healing process.

In conclusion, depression is an essential phase of mourning. It is the moment in which the pain is faced without filters and, through this sadness, a new relationship with the loss begins to be built. Although it is a painful phase, it brings with it the beginning of healing, preparing the mourner to continue on his or her path.

# Welcoming and dealing with sadness

The stage of depression is when the weight of loss becomes more acute. It is a stage characterized by profound sadness, where the world can seem meaningless. Accepting this state of mind is essential to healing.

## Advice:

- **Give yourself permission to be sad**: There is nothing wrong with feeling down. Crying or feeling empty is a natural part of grieving.

- **Avoid total isolation**: Even if you want to be alone, try to maintain contact with a loved one or a professional. Having someone close by can bring you comfort.

- **Take small steps**: Don't try to do too much at this stage. Take the time to do even small daily things, like going for a walk or preparing a meal.

- **Find a creative outlet**: Writing, drawing, or crafting can be a way to express your grief without feeling overwhelmed.

- **Accept that this state will not last forever**: Even if it seems like the sadness will never end, there will be days when the burden will lighten.

**Without You**

Without you,
the world is an empty shadow,
everything seems distant,
like a dream that vanishes upon awakening.

**A Grey Day**

The sky is gray,
but I don't care.
Even the sun,
today,
couldn't warm
the cold inside me.

## The Infinite Silence

In the silence of the morning
I find only emptiness,
an emptiness that speaks of you,
of what will no longer be.

Every breath weighs like a boulder,
every step is slow,
as if walking
no longer made sense.

Time drags on with me,
tired as my soul,
unable to let go of this absence.

**Without Sense**

Nothing makes sense anymore,
everything has vanished.
I walk in an empty world,
waiting for what will never come.

———————— ✕ ————————

**Invisible Tears**

My tears are invisible,
they no longer fall.
Inside me,
the sea is dry,
but the pain remains.

## The Fog of Pain

There is a fog around me,
a mist that envelops everything.
I can't see,
I can't hear.

The world moves,
but I remain still,
lost in this fog,
lost in pain.

Even the sun can't
penetrate this gray,
and all I see
is the void you left.

**An Abyss of Sadness**

Inside me there is an abyss,
a bottomless pit
that swallows every light.
I let myself fall,
I can't take it anymore.

There is nothing to climb back up,
no light at the end,
only the deep darkness
of a pain that knows no bounds.

**Empty Days**

The days pass,
but I feel them flow
like a slow and silent river,
emptied of all meaning.

## No Tomorrow

There is no tomorrow
in this broken today,
there is no future
in this darkness.

Everything is still,
motionless,
as if time itself
had surrendered.

I can't see beyond this darkness,
I can't imagine
a different day.

Maybe this is how it ends,
with a slow fade
into the night.

## The Weight of Silence

The silence weighs,
crushes every thought.
I want to scream,
but I don't have the strength.

## To sink

I'm sinking,
with no hold,
no hands to grab me.
It's all dark here,
and I don't know if I want to go back up.

## The Void That Does Not Fill

There is a void inside me,
an abyss that nothing can fill.
No matter how much I search,
how much I cry,
the void remains,
cold as the night,
deaf to my every plea.

I tried to ignore it,
to hide it,
but the emptiness follows me everywhere,
like a chained shadow.

Every unsaid word,
every lost embrace,
accumulates in this void.

And I wonder if anything
will ever fill it,
if I will ever find peace
in this infinite space of pain.

## The Empty Room

I remain in the empty room,
your absence is palpable.

Every corner seems to scream
your name,
but silence answers,
cold and distant.

I would like to fill this space
with memories,
but every attempt fails.

You are not here,
and your absence weighs
more than I can bear.

## The Day That Never Comes

I wait for a different day,
a day when the pain
has dissolved.
But that day never comes,
and I remain here,
trapped between the past
and a present I don't recognize.

Every hour is longer than the last,
every minute only brings
a greater weight to bear.

### Ash

All that was,
is now ashes.
I blow on the memory,
but the wind disperses everything.

## A Slow Descent

Every day,
I go further down,
further from the light.
Maybe this is where it will end,
in this endless darkness.

## Like Leaves in the Wind

I feel like leaves in the wind,
carried aimlessly,
without direction.
I don't know where I'm going,
I don't know if I'll ever get there.
All I see
is a faded landscape,
a reflection of what was.

## The Burden of Sadness

Sadness is a burden
I carry every day.
It bends me,
it crushes me,
but I can't get rid of it.
Every step becomes heavier,
every breath more laborious.
I wonder if there will ever be
a moment of respite,
a moment of relief.

But sadness gives no respite,
it is like a shadow that follows my every move,
that obscures every ray of light.
I can't see beyond this burden,
I can't imagine a world
where the pain isn't constant.

And so I keep walking,
even though every step seems futile,
even though every breath
is just another whisper in the void.

## The Darkness That Envelops Me

The darkness envelops me,
holds me tight,
and won't let me go.

I don't try to escape,
there is no light beyond this darkness.
I stay here,
hoping for an exit
that I know will never come.

## Deep Solitude

There is no one here,
only my loneliness
filling every corner
of my heart.

*How did you experience the sense of emptiness and sadness that accompanies this phase? In what moments did you feel most vulnerable?*

_____

_____

_____

_____

_____

_____

*Have you ever felt overwhelmed by loneliness, even in the presence of other people?*
*How did you deal with this isolation?*

_____

_____

_____

_____

_____

*Were there any activities or relationships that you abandoned during this phase?*
*How has grief affected your daily life?*

_____

_____

_____

_____

_____

_____

*Have you found ways to express your sadness, such as crying or writing? What has offered you relief, even temporarily, during this time?*

_____

_____

_____

_____

_____

_____

103

*Have you ever tried to suppress or hide your sadness to appear stronger to others? If so, how did this choice affect your healing process?*

*What helped you begin to see a light beyond the depression? Was there a moment when you began to feel that, despite the pain, you could continue to live?*

# Meditation exercise:
# A light in the void

- Close your eyes and imagine that you are in a dark room. This room represents your pain and the emptiness you feel.

- In the center of the room, imagine a small candle lit. The flame is fragile, but constant.

- Inhale deeply and repeat, *"There is light, even if it is small."* Exhale and let the flame grow a little brighter.

- Bring your attention to the light. It is warm and welcoming. Imagine that this light represents a happy memory of your loved one.

- With each breath, let the room gradually lighten, not to erase the darkness, but to make room for serenity.

- When you are ready, open your eyes and bring with you the awareness that even in the deepest darkness, there is always a small light.

"*I have learned that
one does not forget,
but finds peace in remembering,
and the light filters
through the cracks in the heart.*"

# Acceptance

# Recognizing pain and beginning healing

Acceptance, the fifth and final stage of grief, marks the moment when one begins to come to terms with the reality of the loss. It does not mean "getting over" the pain or forgetting who was lost, but learning to live with the new reality. After the emotional turmoil of the previous stages, acceptance brings with it a sense of peace, even if tinged with sadness. One stops fighting against reality and begins to rebuild a new life, integrating the pain.

Unlike the other stages, acceptance is a gradual and often silent process. You slowly come to understand that, despite the pain, life can go on. It is not about eliminating the pain, but about finding a way to make room for the loss, welcoming it as part of your history. In this stage, mourning becomes less acute, evolving into a more stable form of awareness.

Acceptance is not a passive surrender, but an act of inner strength. It involves the recognition that life has changed forever, but also the will to move forward. You no longer try to deny or fight reality, nor find ways to escape. You accept that loss is part of your existence, and you commit to living with this new burden.

Many people, during acceptance, begin to experience a sense of relief. Not actual happiness, but an emotional lightness. You stop looking for impossible answers or solutions, finding a certain relief in accepting what cannot be changed. Loss is no longer a battle, but a reality that can be accepted.

A fundamental aspect of acceptance is reconstruction. You begin to make decisions and make plans for the future. Even though the loved one is no longer present, a new balance is found. The memory of the deceased is integrated into daily life, without the pain paralyzing every action. It is a time of reopening to the world, in which relationships and daily activities resume their place.

It is important to remember that acceptance is not a final goal. There will still be moments of relapse into grief, especially on special occasions such as anniversaries or anniversaries. However, acceptance allows you to face these moments with greater serenity, using the emotional tools developed during the grieving process.

One of the most beautiful aspects of acceptance is the new perspective on life. Loss teaches profound lessons about the fragility and preciousness of existence. Many people, after grieving, develop greater gratitude for the things they have and the people they love. This change in perspective does not erase the pain, but it transforms it, making the person more aware and resilient.

At this stage, you can also begin to celebrate the memory of your loved one in a different way. If the memory was previously a source of pain, during acceptance it becomes a source of comfort. You can reflect on the happy moments you shared without them being overshadowed by pain. Many people find personal ways to honor the memory of their loved one, through rituals or commemorative activities.

Acceptance also allows you to forgive yourself. After experiencing guilt and regret, you come to understand that you could not control the situation. Self-forgiveness is a fundamental step in the healing process, bringing with it compassion and understanding.

The pain of acceptance is different from that of the previous stages: less overwhelming, more subtle, living with a new serenity. Those who have reached this stage often describe a feeling of inner peace. You stop asking "why" and accept reality for what it is.

For those who support a grieving person, acceptance may seem like a positive sign, but it is important to remember that the pain does not go away. The person may still need support and understanding, as acceptance does not erase the loss, but it makes it more manageable. Being present, listening, and offering affection are gestures that continue to make a difference.

Over time, acceptance allows you to find new meaning in your life. Despite the loss, you rediscover joy in small moments and can build new bonds. You continue to grow, carrying the memory of your loved one as an integral part of your story.

In conclusion, acceptance is not a point of arrival, but a new beginning. It is the moment in which one finds the strength to live a life that, even if it includes the pain of loss, can be enriched by new meanings and new experiences. It is a phase of growth and transformation, in which pain turns into wisdom and the memory of the loved one becomes a source of strength.

# Learning to live with pain

Acceptance is not about forgetting or "getting over" the loss, but about recognizing that life can go on, even after the loss. It is the stage where you learn to live with the pain and find new meaning in life.

## Advice:

- **Find new meaning**: Seek out new activities, relationships, or projects that bring you joy and fulfillment. It's not about replacing the person you lost, but about finding new reasons to keep going.

- **Honor the Memory**: Find ways to keep your loved one's memory alive. This could be through rituals, like lighting a candle, or making a donation in their name.

- **Focus on what gives you strength**: Whether it's your family, friends, or personal passions, try to focus on what helps you feel better.

- **Accept that healing is an ongoing process**: There will be good days and hard days, even after you reach acceptance. There is no final finish line.

- **Talk Openly About Your Journey**: Sharing your experience can help both you and others going through similar grief. Talking about grief is part of healing.

**A New Dawn**

A silent dawn,
embraces me with its light.
It doesn't take away the pain,
but it reminds me that there is still life
to be lived,
to be discovered.

**Finding Peace**

There is no end to the memory,
but there is peace in its embrace.
I stay with you,
even as I move on.

## The Strength to Continue

I continue walking,
with my heart slightly more serene.
Every step brings me closer
to a peace I never thought existed.

I haven't forgotten you,
you're with me in every breath,
but now I can look forward,
without feeling the oppressive weight
of your absence.

There is still pain,
but there is also strength,
the strength to continue.

**Accepting the Void**

I didn't fill the void,
but I learned to walk alongside it.
The void doesn't scare me anymore,
it's part of me now.

———— ∞ ————

**The Memory that Guides**

The memory of you no longer crushes me,
now it guides me.
It is a dim light,
a flame that never goes out,
that illuminates my path,
even when everything seems dark.
You are not completely gone,
you have become part of me,
part of my strength.

## Acceptance is a Whisper

Acceptance is a whisper,
not a shout.

It arrives slowly,
like a light wind
that carries away
the last leaves of winter.

There is no fuss,
just a quiet awareness that,
despite everything,
life goes on.

And now
I am ready to follow her,
without fear anymore.

**Beyond the Pain**

Beyond the pain,
I found a way.
It doesn't erase the past,
but it allows me to live again,
to hope again.

**A Smile in Silence**

Now I can smile,
even in the silence of your absence.
It's not a goodbye,
but a see you later.

**Accepting Time**

Time waits for no one,
and I don't want to be left behind any longer.
I walk with it,
with you in my heart.

117

## A New Light

Now I see a new light,
no longer dazzling,
but warm and reassuring.

It is the light of your memory,
which does not hurt,
but accompanies.

You are still a part of me,
in every decision,
in every smile.

You are no longer
an open wound,
you are a scar
that lights my path.

## The Weight Melts Off

The weight of your absence
has not disappeared,
but it has transformed.
It has become lighter,
more bearable.
I carry it with me,
not as a chain,
but as a caress
that reminds me who I was,
who we were.

## Walking Again

The world goes on,
and I walk with it.
I do not forget,
but I find new strength.

## Pain and Peace

The pain has not disappeared,
but it has softened,
like a wound that heals
without ever completely closing.

It remains a mark,
a permanent memory,
but now I can touch it
without feeling that sharp burning
that consumed me at the beginning.

There is peace,
in this pain.

There is peace in accepting
that life goes on,
even without you.

And now I know
that I can carry your memory
without it crushing me,
without it stopping me.

## The Scar That Speaks About Us

I carry a scar with me,
not visible to others,
but clear to me.

It is the trace of what we were,
of what I have lost.

But now it is no longer an open wound,
it is a scar that speaks of us,
of what we have experienced together.

And even though it still burns sometimes,
it reminds me that I can move on,
that I can still live,
without losing what we were.

**Living With**

You don't get over it,
you live with it.
Your absence is part of me,
but it doesn't stop me anymore.
I can look to the future
with new eyes,
even if your memory
remains there,
like a silent presence
that accompanies me.

**Rebirth**

From this pain,
a silent rebirth.
I'm not the same,
but I'm stronger.

## Time Heals

Time does not erase,
but heals slowly,
like a wound that closes
without ever completely disappearing.
Now I can breathe
without the oppressive weight of pain,
the memory remains,
but life resumes its course.

## The Quiet of the Heart

The heart finds peace,
even in pain.
And I find peace
in this new balance.

## A Path of Light

I walked in the dark,
for a long time.
I lost my way,
I stopped,
but now I see a distant light.

It's not brilliant,
it's not immediate,
but it guides me.
It is the light of awareness,
of acceptance.

I have learned that there is no complete healing,
but there is a way to live
with the pain,
without being crushed by it.

Every step brings me closer
to a peace that seemed impossible,
a peace that does not mean forgetting,
but remembering without suffering.

## The Sea and the Wind

I am like the sea,
moved by the wind of memories.

But now,
the wind doesn't overwhelm me,
it guides me.

Every wave that crashes
brings with it a fragment of the past,
but it is no longer painful.

It's just part of the journey,
part of who I've become.

And I continue to sail,
carrying your memory with me,
like a silent compass
that guides me to new shores.

*When did you start to feel like you were reaching some form of acceptance? Was there a specific moment or was it a gradual process?*

_____

_____

_____

_____

_____

*How have you integrated the loss into your daily life?*
*What rituals or activities have helped you honor the memory of your loved one?*

_____

_____

_____

_____

_____

*Have you discovered new meaning or perspective in your life after accepting the loss?*
*How has this experience changed you?*

*How did you find the courage to move forward, even though you carried the pain with you?*
*What gave you the strength to start rebuilding your life?*

*How have you managed to keep the memory of your loved one alive, while accepting their absence? Have you found a balance between remembering and moving on?*

_____

_____

_____

_____

_____

_____

*What does "accepting" loss mean to you?*

*How do you define the concept of acceptance, and how do you experience it in your daily life?*

_____

_____

_____

_____

_____

_____

# Meditation exercise:
# The garden of peace

- Sit down and close your eyes. Breathe slowly, bringing your attention to the rhythm of your heart.

- Imagine walking through a beautiful garden, full of flowers and lush plants. This garden represents your life today, with pain, but also with growth.

- Find a quiet corner of the garden where there is a bench. Sit down and feel the warmth of the sun on your skin.

- Repeat to yourself: "*I have not forgotten, but I have learned to live with my pain.*"

- Inhale slowly and think of a happy memory with your loved one. Exhale and let go of the need to change the past.

- When you are ready, get up from the bench and continue walking in the garden, knowing that, step by step, you can live with strength and serenity.

# A message for you

*Sometimes, the words we couldn't say live on inside us. This is your chance to write a special message for someone who is no longer here. You can share your thoughts, your memories, or simply whatever you feel in your heart. These pages are a space just for you, where the bond with those you love can live on through words.*

# Conclusion

The path of grief is long and complex, made up of stages that pass through the soul and the heart. In this book we have explored the five stages of grief through poetry, a medium that gives voice to emotions that often do not find expression in everyday life. The stages of denial, anger, negotiation, depression and acceptance represent fragments of a painful but necessary path to arrive at a new understanding of life and loss. Grief is not something to be "overcome," but an essential part of the human experience. You never completely leave the pain of a loss behind, but you learn to live with it and integrate it into your existence. Each person experiences grief in a unique way, and there is no right or wrong way to deal with it. This book does not pretend to offer definitive answers, but rather to open a space for reflection and comfort through the power of poetry.

The reflective questions that accompany each stage are an invitation to explore your emotions, to give form to the pain and to find meaning in the midst of suffering. Writing, reflecting and reading can be part of the healing process, helping you to better understand yourself and your relationship with the person you have lost. Even if the pain never goes away completely, every fragment of light you find along the way helps you to see the world with new eyes, discovering that, despite everything, there is still room for hope, love and serenity.

"**Beyond the stars**" is not a linear path to healing, but a collection of moments, reflections and slow steps that allow you to accept pain as part of you. Each stage of grief transforms you, and the poems you have read in these pages are reflections of the complexity of the emotions that grief brings with it.

There is no definitive finish line, nor a perfect end to grief. There are only the steps we continue to take, day after day. Although at first the loss may seem unbearable, over time we learn that it is possible to live, even grow, carrying with us the memory and love of those who are no longer physically present, but continue to live in our hearts.

If there is one final message this book wants to convey, it is that you are not alone. The pain of grief can feel isolating, but it is an experience shared by all of us. Through poetry, reflection, and acceptance, we hope to have offered a space where you can feel understood and welcomed in your grief. Even in the darkest of times, there is always a light, however small, that can guide you toward new awareness and inner peace.

Thank you for taking this journey. May every bit of light you find in these pages illuminate your future path.

If you liked the book
but above all
if it helped you,
leave me a review

Made in the USA
Las Vegas, NV
13 December 2024

14077754R10075